Praise for the *Ear*

There is no doubt that this world is in crisis. The ecological and sociological reality we're living in and must face up to is quite frankly terrifying. Yet there is hope. The authors of the *Earth Spirit* series from Moon Books show us that there are solutions to be found in ecological and eco-spiritual practices. I recommend this series to anyone who is concerned about our current situation and wants to find some hope in solutions they can practice for themselves.
Sarah Kerr, Pagan Federation President

This bold and rich *Earth Spirit* series provides vital information, perspectives, poetry and wisdom to guide and support through the complex environmental, climate and biodiversity challenges and crisis facing us all. Nothing is avoided within the wide range of author views, expertise and recommendations on eco-spirituality. I am deeply inspired by the common call, across the books, to radically change our relationship with the planet to a more respectful, mutual, spiritual and sustainable way of living; both individually and collectively. Each book offers its own particular flavour and practical offering of solutions and ways forward in these unprecedented times. Collectively the series provides an innovative, inspiring and compelling compendium of how to live, hope and act from both ancient and modern wisdoms. Whatever your views, concerns and aspirations for your life, and for the planet, you will find something of value. My life and understanding is deeply enhanced through the privilege of reading this series.
Dr Lynne Sedgmore CBE, Founder of Goddess Luminary Leadership Wheel, Executive Coach, Priestess and ex Chief Executive

In a world that is faced with such immense environmental issues, we can often feel paralysed and impotent. The *Earth Spirit* series is a welcome and inspiring antidote to fear and apathy. These books gift us with positive and inspiring visions that serve to empower and strengthen our own resolve to contribute to the healing of our planet, our communities and ourselves.

Eimear Burke, Chosen Chief of The Order of Bards, Ovates and Druids

Thanks to Moon Books and an amazing group of authors for stepping up in support of our need to address, with grace and aliveness, the ecological crises facing humanity. We must take concerted, focused, positive action on every front NOW, and this is best and most powerfully done when we base our offerings in a deep sense of spirit. White Buffalo Woman came to us 20 generations ago, reminding us of the importance of a holy perception of the world - based in Oneness, unity, honor and respect. Even as that is profound, it is also practical, giving us a baseline of power from which to give our gifts of stewardship and make our Earth walk a sacred one - for us and for All Our Relations. Walk in Beauty with these authors!

Brooke Medicine Eagle, Earthkeeper and author of *Buffalo Woman Comes Singing* and *The Last Ghost Dance*

Earth Spirit is an exciting and timely series. It has never been more important to engage with ideas that promote a positive move forward for our world. Our planet needs books like these - they offer us heartening signposts through the most challenging of times.

Philip Carr-Gomm, author of *Druid Mysteries, Druidcraft* and *Lessons in Magic*

This is important work as we humans face one of the greatest challenges in our collective history.

Ellen Evert Hopman, Archdruid of Tribe of the Oak and author of *A Legacy of Druids, A Druid's Herbal of Sacred Tree Medicine, The Sacred Herbs of Spring,* and other volumes

Our relationship to the Mother Earth and remembering our roles as caretakers and guardians of this sacred planet is essential in weaving ourselves back into the tapestry of our own sacred nature. From the shamanic perspective, we are not separate from nature. The journey to finding solutions for the Earth will come through each person's reconnection to her heartbeat and life force.

Chandra Sun Eagle, author of *Looking Back on the Future*

What people are saying about

Saving Mother Ocean

Steve Andrews understands that the key to defending and protecting life and diversity in the Ocean is to use what you are good at to find solutions to seemingly impossible problems. The strength of an eco-system depends upon diversity and interdependence. Therefore, a successful movement is defined by diversity and interdependence within it. By harnessing our passions to the virtues of courage and imagination we can find impossible solutions to seemingly impossible problems. *Saving Mother Ocean* is inspiring, informative and a call to action by all of us to save the Mother to all of us – the Ocean.
Captain Paul Watson, Founder of the Sea Shepherd Conservation Society

Lots of facts and background information and your journey. I think people will find it very informative as you tell it straight! The ocean is life, we must protect it.
Lily Platt, Global Youth Ambassador, Speaker and Environmental Champion

It is a thorough and properly alarming review of the many threats that we have created to the life in and of the oceans. Our fate depends on the health of the seas, and we need to open our eyes to what is happening.
Alan Ereira, filmmaker, author and historian

Where Does all The Plastic Go? Into the sea, into the sea! Sing along while reading this fabulous book *Saving Mother Ocean* by Steve Andrews. Find out who first discovered plastic pollution in the Pacific Ocean and how Andrews got inspired to become an

ocean advocate by a plastic catamaran also known as the Plastiki. Andrews is a pioneer in raising awareness and motivating others to become change makers. This is an excellent book for anyone who wants to be informed about plastic pollution and who wants to make a difference. Thank you, Steve Andrews, for inspiring thousands to protect our planet mother ocean.
Janina Rossiter, artist, ocean advocate and award-winning author

Steve Andrews continues on his remarkable journey by focusing our attention on the Earth's Oceans and what can be done to clean up our act of living here. I'm honored to be mentioned and inspired to devote more of my time to eco-activism, especially actions caring for our Mother Ocean.
Stephen Friedland, singer and songwriter

A wake up call for the world - if this book doesn't make you think differently nothing will.
Mike Kennedy, Director MADACP Global SWND

Knowledgeable, energetic, eclectic, Steve Andrews' writing is always a delight. The subject is worrying, but the book also includes at least the suggestion of a solution, in the form of Ocean Aid, Steve's grand vision for an awareness-raising campaign to bring the plight of the oceans to the world's attention.
C. J. Stone, author and journalist

A remarkable insight into the international threats towards the natural earth, its oceans and its land, along with the outstanding explanation of the author's efforts to create Ocean Aid to provide relief and conservation to all marine life.
Jack Ellis-Leek, WEAW Founder

Through a combination of prose and poetry, Andrews highlights the sad plight of our oceans and offers some suggestions about what we can do to turn this dire situation around. It's not a long book, but it is worth reading if you wish to gain a better understanding of what is happening to the oceans and why.

Luke Eastwood, author of *How to Save The Planet'* and *The Journey*

Earth Spirit
Saving Mother Ocean

Steve Andrews

EARTH SPIRIT
Saving Mother Ocean

Steve Andrews

MOON
BOOKS
Winchester, UK
Washington, USA

JOHN HUNT PUBLISHING

First published by Moon Books, 2021
Moon Books is an imprint of John Hunt Publishing Ltd., No. 3 East Street, Alresford
Hampshire SO24 9EE, UK
office@jhpbooks.net
www.johnhuntpublishing.com
www.moon-books.net

For distributor details and how to order please visit the 'Ordering' section on our website.

ISBN: 978 1 78904 965 7
978 1 78904 966 4 (ebook)
Library of Congress Control Number: 2021938950

A CIP catalogue record for this book is available from the British Library.

Design: Matthew Greenfield

UK: Printed and bound by CPI Group (UK) Ltd, Croydon, CR0 4YY
Printed in North America by CPI GPS partners

We operate a distinctive and ethical publishing philosophy in
all areas of our business, from our global network of authors to
production and worldwide distribution.

Contents

Introduction   1

Mother Earth, Mother Ocean and Neptune   3
Ocean Aid   12
Down the River into the Sea   21
Threats to the Oceans   27
Ocean Meadows and Forests in the Sea   45
Action We Can Take   51
Let the Children Lead Us   58
Organisations Helping to Save the Oceans   61

Suggested Further Reading   65
About the Author   66

"If the ocean dies, we die."
Captain Paul Watson, Sea Shepherd

Introduction

We associate beaches with summer days, with holidays and happiness, while the mighty oceans have long inspired authors, poets and painters. But today the seas are in very real danger. Nowadays, the oceans and the marine life in them are seriously threatened, and so are we, because we depend on healthy seas. Plastic pollution continues daily, and I am sure you have all seen the alarming reports, as well as the disgusting mess on beaches where washed up plastic flotsam has become the new normal. Overfishing is decimating stocks of fish worldwide too. Whales are dying, often 'beaching' themselves, and autopsies reveal masses of plastic in the stomachs of these majestic sea mammals. Turtles and seabirds are in trouble too. The news of marine wildlife these days is seldom good news. It is clear that all is not well!

A big part of the problem and the reason this environmental nightmare has happened, is that humans have been treating the ocean as an endless expanse of water, a place they can fish for a limitless supply of food, and a place that can be used as the limitless garbage dump for the whole world. We are learning swiftly, and it is a very great shame, we didn't learn a lot sooner, that there are limits to the oceans. We cannot keep taking whatever we want from them. We cannot keep dumping our trash, and anything we don't want, in the oceans, thinking whatever it was we no longer had use for, had gone away and would be safely disposed of by the mighty oceans. There was and is no gone away! The oceans, like this planet, have boundaries when it comes to their size and what they can hold. The oceans are finite. Yet, at the same time, the oceans all run into each other somewhere, so, in many ways, there is only one ocean.

I am a naturalist and have been since I was a little boy, who discovered the beauty and magic of nature at an early age, and my connection with the natural world has stayed with me all the way through my life. Because of this I regard myself as very lucky, but I have become increasingly worried about the natural world. I have been watching the destruction continue for many years, and in the last decade or so it has become so terrible, so depressing, so frightening, that I felt I had to do something. I became an activist and conservationist. You have no doubt seen Greta Thunberg and environmentalists, talking about how we need to take action now. She is usually talking about the Climate Crisis and that is the most serious of all the problems we face, and it also has a strong impact on the crisis in the seas as well. I agree with Greta that we need action now, not tomorrow, next week, next month, next year, by 2030, by 2050.... but NOW! Besides being an activist, I am also a writer, and one action I knew I could take was to write about what is happening in the hopes of raising awareness and inspiring change.

When Trevor Greenfield, the Publisher of Moon Books, decided to publish an *Earth Spirit* series of books devoted to eco-spirituality and wanted someone to offer a title on saving the oceans, and I knew it had to be me. I was already focused on doing this. I was already actively campaigning to save the seas. Happily, he agreed. So, in this book, I am going to be taking a look at the threats to the oceans, and sadly there are a lot more than plastic pollution and overfishing, but more about these other dangers later on. First of all, let us take a look at how saving the oceans can be considered from an eco-spiritual viewpoint and why we should be thinking of the oceans as our Mother. She is the source of all life and we need to take care of Her!

Mother Earth, Mother Ocean, and Neptune

Many people think of our home planet as "Mother Earth," a living spiritual being that is the mother of all life, including ourselves. This belief is not only held by a growing number of individuals in modern society but is also held by many indigenous people, who think of a creator who is our mother, as opposed to God the father, of the patriarchal religions. Mother Earth has also come to be widely known as "Gaia," due to the work of best-selling author, environmentalist and scientist James Lovelock. In the 1960s he came up with the "Gaia hypothesis" that puts forward the idea that the planet Earth is a self-regulating living organism. Whatever the truth may really be, many people like to think of this planet as our "Mother." But it was the patriarchal religions with their male god that came to power thousands of years back, and they are the main religions of the world today. And yet, all these powerful religions were only created within the last 6,000 years, a tiny fraction of the length of time the Earth has existed and a tiny fraction of time on which life has lived and evolved on this planet. It is certainly something to think about! We find ourselves today living in a world that has been subjected to patriarchal rules and values. We are living in a world which has followed God's advice in the Old Testament where in Genesis 1:28 it says:

"Be fruitful and multiply and fill the earth and subdue it, and have dominion over the fish of the sea and over the birds of the heavens and over every living thing that moves on the earth."

Now we have an overpopulated planet of over seven billion people, fast approaching eight, and a world in which humans have done what they please with the natural world, a world in which an unimaginable number of "living things" have been subjected to horrific cruelty and death, and continue to be victims of human violence. It is a world in which the extinction of countless species of animals and plants are happening. So "business as usual" continues at present with devastating results. Admittedly when that scripture was written thousands of years back the planet did not have the billions of people living on it that it does today, but it has still added to the problems of the world as far as I am concerned. It has given us the idea that we are more important than any other animal, and this goes some of the way to explaining why humans are so often speciesist.

However, I am not going to go any further in discussing patriarchal religions here because this is not what this book is about, but I do feel it is important to consider the role these religious beliefs have had over so many people and societies of the 'civilised' world. I put the term civilised in inverted commas because it has been civilisation that has seemingly destroyed so much life. We need to ask ourselves, if civilisation is so wonderful why does it cause so much death and destruction?

It appears this has happened because of the technologies we have developed, technologies that are not bad in themselves but technologies that can have devastating consequences when used unwisely. This is the real problem. I am sure you can think of plenty of examples. Technology has been at the root of human progress through the ages, and this is very good, but technology can also be our downfall. Civilisation and its technological advances could have added to the paradise this world is, but, tragically it has often had the opposite effect. I was thinking about these matters and realised that "Mother Ocean" made a lot of sense when giving a name for the source of life on our planetary home, and hence the title of this book. After all, the oceans are where all life began. Science has established this and scientists also are very aware that life on this planet depends on a healthy ocean. One of the main reasons is the role that oceans play in keeping the gases in the atmosphere in balance. The ongoing Climate Crisis is due to an imbalance with greenhouse gases having risen to dangerous levels. This has been caused by human activity with the burning of fossil fuels one of the most serious contributors to the problem. Carbon dioxide is one of the gases causing the most harm. There is simply too much of it in the atmosphere.

In a healthy scenario the oceans absorb a lot of this gas, as do the forests. 70% of the world is covered in water and 97% of it is in the oceans. The oceans have such an important role in keeping a correct balance of gases in the atmosphere by absorbing carbon dioxide. According to legendary oceanographer Sylvia Earle, the ocean is the "biggest carbon sink on the planet."

The oceans also play a major role in regulating heat. The topmost metres of the sea store as much heat as the atmosphere above. However, in a warming ocean the life that lives there must either tolerate the temperatures, adapt, move or die. In the very unhealthy situation the world is in today the forests are being lost to developments, logging and to wildfires, so they are unable to carry on their function as the "lungs of the planet." Meanwhile the oceans are absorbing the excess carbon dioxide causing acidification of the sea water and serious damage to many forms of marine life that depend on calcium being available in the water, and the water not being acidic. Many forms of marine life thrive in a slightly alkaline water, and this they no longer have in many parts of the seas.

Getting back to the idea of the Mother, as the Creator, as Mother Earth, as Mother Ocean, the Kogi people of Columbia, very much believe that this world and everything in it was originally thought of, and thus created by Aluna, their name for the Great Mother. These indigenous people are the descendants of the ancient Tairona. They live on the Sierra Nevada de Santa Marta, a mountain range they think of as the "Heart of the World." They have managed to keep their culture intact, because over 500 years ago, when they were invaded by the Spanish, they retreated up the mountains out of the way of their attackers. In escaping from the Spanish would-be conquerors, the Kogi were able to continue living as they had always done and to preserve their spiritual beliefs and ceremonies.

The Kogi believe that long long ago after this world had been created that they were given the job of being guardians for the rest of the world and that their sacred mountain home is the heart of the planet. They call it "Gonawindua". The other tribal people known as the Wiwa, Arhuaco and Kankuamo, who also live on the Sierra Nevada de Santa Marta mountain range, have very similar beliefs and culture.

The spiritual leaders of the Kogi are known as Mamos or Mamas, meaning "enlightened ones." They dress only in white to show their purity and like to go barefoot as much as possible to maintain their contact with the Earth. These Mamos are selected by divination as babies. They are kept in semi-darkness for the first nine years of their lives, only being visited by their mothers and by Mamos who help instruct them. The nine years they remain like this are like the nine months of pregnancy. When the Mamos-in-training enter the world again it is like being reborn and they get to see the wonders that the Great Mother has created and that they have heard about in their years of instruction.

Mamos believe they were entrusted with the sacred task of performing special ceremonies and tasks for the benefit of all life on Earth. An important part of this is the giving back of gifts to Mother Earth. If we take from the planet, we must give something back. They believe too that the 'civilised' peoples of the world are their "Younger Brother." They believe that when the Younger Brother was first created, he caused so many problems that one of the Great Mother's first children, a deity known as Serankwa, sent the Younger Brother away across the ocean, and gave him knowledge of machines (technology). This was after the Younger Brother had refused to listen and was ripping at the earth, much as he is still doing today. The idea was for the Kogi Mamos to be able to continue their work in peace from the Heart of the World, protected from the troublesome and destructive Younger Brother.

This all worked well for them, and all was peaceful, until the Spanish arrived bringing with them the Catholic religion, guns and death, and so the Kogi retreated, they ran for their lives. Since then, they have kept themselves secluded from the Younger Brother's world that they are able to see in the lower levels of the mountain and along the coast. The Kogi were well aware that the Younger Brother had continued in his destructive ways but they did not interfere. They do not have anger or any bad feelings towards the Younger Brother, because they recognise him as their brother, who was created to live here but they are greatly saddened and frustrated by his actions.

The Mamos believe they must care for all living things. They have a very great understanding of ecology and how a healthy ecosystem should be. They have the amazing reality of living on a mountain chain that provides a microcosm to the rest of the world as the macrocosm. This is because every microclimate and environmental habitat exists somewhere between the coast and the summits. However, the Mamos knew that something was very badly wrong because the mountain peak no longer had ice and snow on the tundra, and the clouds that bring rainfall were no longer present. They know that if there are no clouds and no snow and ice at the higher levels then there will be no water for the lower parts and that whatever lives there will die without it.

So worried about this were the Kogi Mamos that in 1990 they decided they would break their silence and would talk to the Younger Brother in the outside world. They allowed filmmaker Alan Ereira to travel into Kogi territory, to film them and to make a documentary for the *BBC* with the title of *From the Heart of The World: The Elder Brother's Warning*. In it everything I have explained here is described in much greater detail and their warning is made. The Kogi say that if we, the Younger Brother, do not stop drilling, mining, extracting minerals and ripping away the Mother's body that the world will come to an end some day in the future, and they will no longer be able to stop this. They explain that the Mother is very sad and that she feels great pain from what humans are doing to her body. They predicted that new illnesses will occur and that there will be no medicine. It is as if they were forecasting the Covid-19 pandemic.

In the film, Ereira is shown high on the mountain in a tundra area where vegetation suited to this habitat should be growing but instead, what was there crumbled to dust when touched. This scene is shown before the documentary ends and the director makes the point of telling viewers that this situation on the summit is what finally made the Mamos decide to talk to us. That documentary made a very big impact on me when I saw it back in 1990. Then back in the winter of 2012, when I was living in Tenerife, I went through an experience that was so similar to what had worried the Kogi so much.

It was in January and I had gone up Mt Teide, the highest mountain in Spain, to show a friend who was visiting the island, what it was like up there. I was expecting the highland vegetation to be growing, as it usually does in winter but what was left of the low-growing scrubland bushes was dead or dying. Much of what I went to touch crumbled to dust in my hands. Where there should have been vibrant greenery there was the brown colour of dead vegetation in the barren looking landscape. I knew that this vegetation depends on the autumn and winter rains and snowfall. There had been very little if any.

My mind flashed back to that scene of Ereira on the Sierra Nevada De Santa Marta. The island was experiencing a winter drought as a result of climate change. It was having devastating effects but no one else seemed to be concerned. Tourists were wandering about on the mountain smiling and taking photos. Can't they see the devastation in front of them I wondered to myself? I was working in the media at the time, writing for the newspapers there, but people I knew told me it will all be ok, the rains will soon come, but they were wrong, and Tenerife farmers had a really terrible year with crop failure that year. I knew that what the Kogi Mamos were talking about was a reality, and it has been a motivator for me to take action. But how should I take action? What should I do?

For several years now I have felt a personal calling to do what I can to help save the seas, to help save life in general on this planet. I realised that images would be needed to help my readers understand what I was hoping to convey. I thought of the archetypal and classical god images for the rulers of the oceans. The god Neptune, or Poseidon, as this deity is also known, came to mind. Neptune is a Roman deity and Poseidon is his Greek counterpart. This god is depicted carrying a pronged trident and I thought this image fitted well as a tool on which floating litter in the seas could be speared. I thought of the idea of how we could all be helping Neptune get the plastic and other rubbish out of the oceans. I can think of Neptune as an eco-warrior deity, a god who fights to save his watery domain.

I also thought of how this image has inspired the DC Comics superhero Aquaman, now the hero of the very successful film with the same name. If thinking about a superhero or a god you can be inspired by will help motivate you to take action, then perhaps Neptune and/or Aquaman can be your personal motivator. Neptune and Aquaman are both associated with Atlantis, the continent of legend that went under the seas, many believe because of the wrongdoings of people at the time.

Speaking of Atlantis, at one point in my life, from around 2004 onwards, I was corresponding at great length with the late Professor Arysio Nunes dos Santos from Brazil, who besides holding very impressive academic qualifications in Nuclear Physics, was an expert on Atlantis. He told me that when he first started researching it as a scientist that he was very sceptical, but the further he delved the more he became convinced of its reality. He had researched the languages of the world and the historical spread of people and cultures. He was convinced that he had found enough evidence to prove the existence of Atlantis. He came up with the controversial theory that Atlantis had never been found because people have been looking in the wrong places, and that they had failed to understand Plato's writings about it.

He believed that it is under the South China Sea and that Indonesia is all that is left. He theorised that Atlantis had colonies and cities in what is now India, and that was where civilisation survived. He also believed that there had been previous cultures that gave rise to the belief in Lemuria/Mu. Professor Santos told me that he felt that it was possible that the world was heading in the same direction again as the Atlanteans had taken. He felt he was on a mission to get the world to understand what was happening and that was why he had to make his findings available. The book *Atlantis, the Lost Continent Finally Found* explains the basics of his research and conclusions. He believed the Atlanteans had nuclear power and that it had contributed to their downfall. He also felt that the Biblical Garden of Eden was a memory of Atlantean times.

Whether he was right or wrong with his ideas about Atlantis, it has also been theorised by other writers and thinkers that the Biblical story of the Flood as God's punishment for a sinful world was based on Atlantis going under the waves. With the predicted sea level rise being created by the melting polar ice we seem to be having a similar situation being created today. Greenland, glaciers and the ice at both poles has been melting at an alarming rate, and the permafrost in Siberia is thawing. If the sea levels keep rising it has been predicted that coastal cities will be drowned, which would mean the end of civilization as we know it.

I must admit that much of what I have just been talking about in this chapter has been speculation, theories, and beliefs; nothing that stands up to laboratory tests or is found in peer-reviewed journals. However, modern scientists have become increasingly worried about the state of the planet and what the future holds too. Scientists are very concerned about the melting polar ice. Climate Change too had long been predicted by science. But bearing all this in mind, whether we choose to look at the problem from a spiritual and esoteric point of view or from a scientific one, it is obvious we are in deep trouble. It really shouldn't matter anymore what you believe. Everyone that lives on the planet, whether they are adherents of a particular religion or sect, or whether they are non-believers, atheists or agnostics, they still depend on the health of the oceans and the ecosystem of the world. So, whatever way you want to think about our planet and how it was created is not the issue, what is important is whether we can reverse the way the world looks very likely to be heading.

I knew I had to try to do whatever I could! I hope that with this book I can inspire you too!

Ocean Aid

My understanding of how serious the plastic pollution problem really is began back in 2010 when I started following the work of explorer, author and environmentalist, David de Rothschild, who at the time was sailing a plastic catamaran known as the Plastiki across the Pacific Ocean. De Rothschild's boat was made from 12,500 reclaimed plastic bottles and other recycled plastic and his voyage was aimed at raising awareness about how we should be recycling plastic, and about the problems in the oceans today. He planned with his crew to sail past the Great Pacific Garbage Patch, a mind-bogglingly massive area of mainly floating plastic pieces, so big that it has been estimated to be the size of Texas. It is what is known as a "gyre", and there are actually five of these accumulations of floating garbage in the oceans of the world.

The Plastiki sailed from San Francisco to Sydney and the trials and tribulations endured on the voyage, as well as the rewarding experiences and findings of de Rothschild and his crew, are collected together in his book entitled *Plastiki Across the Pacific on Plastic: An Adventure to Save Our Oceans*. The Plastiki had been made as a tribute of sorts to the Kon-Tiki, the raft that the world explorer, the late Thor Heyerdahl, had built and sailed in making headlines in his time. Heyerdahl had kept a record of the incredible amount of marine life seen along the route of the Kon-Tiki's voyage, but in contrast the crew of The Plastiki were depressed to see very few seabirds, fish or whales. This point is made in the book to show how much the plight of the oceans had worsened in such a comparatively short space of time.

Guest writers were included in de Rothschild's book and one of these was Captain Charles J. Moore. An oceanographer, Captain Moore is one of the main people to have done what he can to bring the grim reality of the plastic pollution problem into the public arena. He is credited as having drawn the world's attention to the Great Pacific Garbage patch in 1997. In an essay for *Natural History,* he wrote:

> "In the week it took to cross the subtropical high, no matter what time of day I looked, plastic debris was floating everywhere: bottles, bottle caps, wrappers, fragments."

He had also discovered a beach in Hawaii, which is so badly polluted with plastic waste that much of what appears to be sand is actually tiny particles of microplastic. Moore founded Algalita Marine Research and Education, and later on, in May 2020, went on to found The Moore Institute for Plastic Pollution Research, of which he is the Research Director. Finding out the reality of the extent of the plastic nightmare scenario inspired me to write a poem, which was later to become the lyrics for my song *Where Does All the Plastic Go?* I also thought, wouldn't it be great if

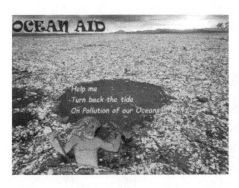

someday we could have an Ocean Aid concert, just like the earlier Live Aid, but this time raising awareness about the plight of the oceans and raising funds for charities helping to save the seas? I envisaged world famous bands and pop singers being involved and the concert to be held in a stadium somewhere with plenty of media coverage. It was a big dream. It still is! However, saving the oceans is a very big task, one of the biggest I can think of! But it has to be done!

Getting back to my song, it had remained a poem for some years, and I was waiting for someone famous to start singing about the problems in the oceans. I realised, of course, that we don't hear protest songs like back in the late 1960s when many of these sorts of song actually became hits, but there are still singer-songwriters writing in this genre. One of them is Neil Young, and he happens to be one of my main musical mentors and heroes. Young has been writing protest songs all the way through his career. In the last decade or so he has been outspoken in his material and in a wide range of topics. On his album *Living With War,* he wrote of the dangers of consumerism in *The Restless Consumer*, and went as far as calling for the removal of George Bush as POTUS in *Let's Impeach the President*. More recently he brought out an album entitled *The Monsanto Years*, and has campaigned both in song and in person against the tar sands in Canada and the oil pipeline in Dakota. But even Young was not protesting about plastic pollution. It looked as if it was being left up to me to do this. And so, in 2017, I came up with a tune to go with my words and the song *Where Does All the Plastic Go?* was born.

I had begun working with Jayce Lewis as my producer at his Northstone Studios in Bridgend, south Wales, and he produced my protest song about plastic pollution. Photographer Filipe Rafael helped film and create a video for the song back in Portugal. The video shows footage of me in the beautiful countryside contrasted against clips showing plastic pollution. Now, I admit that I have heard a wide range of very famous singers and musicians talking about plastic and the problem it has become. Mick Jagger, Brian May, Cerys Matthews, Chrissie Hynde and Kanye West have all done so, but as far as I know I am leading the way when it comes to songs about the subject.

Where Does All the Plastic Go?

Plastic plants, what about real plants?
I saw the fake ones at the store,
People must want them,
People must buy them,
I don't want to see any more.

Where does all the plastic go?
Into the sea, into the sea,
How does it get there,
Who threw it away,
Was it you or was it me?

It's not hunting that will kill the last whale,
Plastic will do it and it's a very sad tale,
And all the albatrosses are dying out too,
They keep on fishing in the ocean's plastic stew.

Where does all the plastic go?
Into the sea, into the sea,
How does it get there,
Who threw it away,
Was it you or was it me?

The plastic bag I bought,
It very quickly broke,
And if it ever gets burned,
There'll be poisonous smoke.

Where does all the plastic go?
Into the sea, into the sea,
How does it get there,
Who threw it away,
Was it you or was it me?

Plastic kills the turtles,
And it's eaten by the fish,
Plastics in the food-chain,
And the dinner on your dish.

Where does all the plastic go?
Into the sea, into the sea,
How does it get there,
Who threw it away,
Was it you or was it me?

I decided I needed as much publicity as I could get for my song and my Ocean Aid concert idea. It has become my main focus, so writing this book is perfect for me, and what I was already doing this year. I have been getting some great coverage in the media. Examples include being on the front page of *The Portugal News* with a caption "Singing against pollution," having an entire 4-page chapter also entitled Where Does all The Plastic Go? in *SPAM Stop Plastica A Mare*, a book by Italian radio host Filippo Solibello, and being featured in *The Wave* magazine, published by The Rotary Club of Wyndham Harbour, from Australia. I have also been featured in the *Gonzo Weekly* talking about my song and ideas, and an Ocean Aid image was used on the cover. *SWND* magazine from Wales also helped spread the word about Ocean Aid in the Spring 2021 edition. I had a feature too in *Whitstable Views* on 8 March, simply titled "Mother Ocean". In April 2021 I was a guest speaker on *WBAI FM* from New York, talking about "Saving the Seas from Plastic"'. I am delighted that I am getting to publicise my song and talk about my ideas to such an international readership and listenership, because the problems in the oceans are international problems. We are going to need a worldwide response from as many people as possible in helping to turn the tide (excuse the pun) on all this.

The Covid-19 pandemic with the lockdowns and restrictions imposed by governments worldwide put a stop to so many normal activities for people everywhere. Musicians found they could no longer play concerts on stages at venues but it soon became realised that one way for music still to be performed was by live-streaming online. This has become a "new norm" at time of writing, and I am one of the many musicians who have been using the marvels of Internet technology to carry on doing what we do. I realised that right now a massive Ocean Aid Concert on a stadium stage somewhere would be out of the question, even if somehow, I had managed to get this happening, if somehow, I had found the sponsors and media backing to make this happen. However, there is no reason that virtual concerts cannot be held, and the more the better.

I realised that if Ocean Aid Concerts could become a worldwide movement that would be a very desirable way forward. Now it is a matter of interest that Solibello had asked me if I minded if he spread the word to his media contacts in Italy with a view to getting Ocean Aid off the ground. I told him, no, it didn't matter to me where Ocean Aid takes place. I just want to see it happen. The Italian radio host, who is famous in his country, was touring to promote his book and tell people about my song and concert idea. He even managed to get a copy of SPAM *Stop Plastica A Mare* to Pope Francis and this was covered in the media. I was going to be invited over to Italy but then the pandemic struck, Italy was one of the first countries to be badly affected, and our plans were put on hold.

However, as already mentioned, I have become one of the many musicians using Zoom and Facebook to take part in events that are streamed live. Over a year ago I began performing as one of the regulars on Rew Starr's ReW & WhO? Show from New York. Starr is a living legend in the American city and so is Stephen Friedland, aka Brute Force[1], who is a regular guest. He once had his song *The King of Fuh* supported by the late John Lennon and George Harrison to the degree that it got released on the Apple label. It was looking as if he had found his really big break but then EMI and Capitol said they were unwilling to distribute his song and it got pulled. It did, however, get released many years after this. Friedland also has a very important album project he calls *Planetwork* and a "Pledge of Allegiance" poster that goes with it. He is making the point that if we think in terms of pledging allegiance to the planet, then artificial boundaries that humans have created, their nationalities and other divisions will fall away.

He is saying we are all living on and dependent on the same planet for our lives and home, and outside this planet there is the universe, which we should pledge allegiance to as well. I agree with so much of what he is saying in his work. Anyway, I decided that I could ask the regulars of Starr's show to support me in the first Ocean Aid Concert, and we held this online on 10 February 2021. James Lane, who is a representative of the

Green Party produces and hosts the ReW & WhO? Show, and he helped me with my concert, and Brute Force and Rew Starr were two of the performers. I decided too that we would collect funds for Captain Paul Watson's Sea Shepherd charity, and there will be more about their work later in this book. So, Ocean Aid has happened as a concert, and I am wishing that many more such events will happen in future. I am hoping that many more people will feel inspired to take action in this way and to help save the oceans with songs and performances that raise awareness. I even came up with a new song entitled *Time for Ocean Aid*. Of course, I started the concert with it.

Time for Ocean Aid
We've got to save the birds, we've got to save the bees,
We've got to save the forests, we've got to save the seas,
When I look at all the mess we've made, I think it's time for ocean aid.
Microplastic pollution is bound to make you think,
It is even in the air and the water that we drink.
The Amazon's burned so much,
Australia's been burning too,
Wildfires are the new normal,
So what are we gonna do?

We've got to save the birds, we've got to save the bees,
We've got to save the forests, we've got to save the seas,
When I look at all the mess we've made, I think it's time for ocean aid.

There's an insect Armageddon,
A sixth great extinction underway,
But keep the economy growing,
There's more jobs I hear them say.

We've got to save the birds, we've got to save the bees,
We've got to save the forests, we've got to save the seas,
When I look at all the mess we've made, I think it's time for
ocean aid.

Where are the real world leaders?
Please tell me where they are,
Those speaking in the media,
Are just talking more blah-blah.

We've got to save the birds, we've got to save the bees,
We've got to save the forests, we've got to save the seas,
When I look at all the mess we've made, I think it's time for
ocean aid.

[1] Brute Force® is a registered trademark of Stephen Friedland
and registered with USPTO.

Down the River into the Sea

In one of my songs, I ask how the plastic gets into the sea, and one of the main ways is down drains, into streams and rivers. From there it is carried to the oceans, unless it gets caught up in overhanging riverbank vegetation where it also badly pollutes the environment. The plastic and other rubbish gets into the waterways in many ways. It isn't simply dumped there. When there are storms that cause flooding the rubbish from streets and countryside ends up in drains and rivers. This is one way that litter creates a very serious problem. It can also cause problems when still inland if animals and birds swallow it or get trapped and entangled in items that have been carelessly discarded. The amount of rubbish washing down to the seas daily is truly alarming. Perhaps you have seen photos or footage, especially from third world countries, in which a river is totally covered in floating plastic?

I remember back when I was living in Tenerife, I helped Dinah McAlees, a science teacher friend there, organise an educational trip to a local beach where the children could see for themselves the amount of plastic that was causing terrible pollution. My friend worked at the Britannia School in Puerto de la Cruz and the beach we chose was one on the northwest coast of the island called La Caleta. We went there to do a recce and I was able to show McAlees how a lot of the plastic had washed down a drain that emptied on the beach from the seaside village above. A lot more plastic was washing up with the tide. I remember showing my friend a small blue plastic bottle and being able to show the visual similarity with a Portuguese man o' war, a floating marine creature that resembles a jellyfish but is actually a hydrozoan or siphonophore and is made up of a colony of polyps. It can be very dangerous to humans because of its stinging tentacles but the Loggerhead Turtle feeds on the Man 'o war. This is where the problem lies for the marine reptile, not because of the stinging power of its floating prey but because it can easily mistake blueish plastic for the float and tentacles of its natural food source.

When the children came to the beach, fortunately, there were no more Portuguese man o' wars present but the amount of plastic they found was shocking. They did surveys of areas on the beach, as well as collecting pieces to take back to school to use in collage and artwork they would be creating. It is not only big marine creatures, such as whales, turtles and fish that are eating plastic because even the microscopic plankton are doing so. The real problem with plastic is that it was made to last and is unable to be broken down into anything but smaller and smaller pieces. Tiny plastic particles are called microplastics and the even smaller ones are nanoplastics. Plankton can feed on plastic when it reaches a microscopic size. Speaking of plankton, they are drastically declining in numbers in many parts of the seas. A study in 1999 by Captain Moore, whom I mentioned earlier, found as many as six parts of plastic to one of plankton. Later research in 2002 discovered a 5:2 ratio of plastic to plankton off the coast of California.

Plastic is just one of many harmful substances that washes down the rivers. Pesticides, toxic chemicals, detergents, slurry from farms and raw sewage are other very serious contaminants of fresh water that end up in the oceans. In the U.S. the amount of run-off from farms has created what have come to be known as "dead zones." Thousands of square miles of coastal sea and seabed are devoid of life because of the terrible amount of pollution carried to them.

In the U.K. and elsewhere pesticides are another major problem, and not just those from farms where they have been sprayed on crops but also the ones used to treat our pet cats and dogs. Flea and tick-killer insecticides cause death not only for these insect pests but for freshwater insects and other invertebrates. Surveys of rivers have not only shown alarming amounts of these chemicals present but an equally alarming decline in once common insects and their larvae, such as mayfly and stonefly nymphs. These insects were and are an essential part of the diet of fish. They are a vital component of the food-chain. If food is lacking fish will starve. Pet dogs out on walks often run into streams and rivers and go splashing around. This is fun for them but sadly if their coats have been treated with insecticide the chemicals can come off in the water.

Slurry, especially from chicken farms, is yet another terrible pollutant of rivers. Some famous ones such as the River Wye that once boasted salmon populations and otters, now are being ruined by the amount of agricultural slurry. This river is on the border of England and Wales but many other waterways in both countries are experiencing this problem and it is leading to mass die-offs of freshwater fish.

You wouldn't expect a river to have raw sewage in it but increasingly the rivers are polluted with this. Tons of untreated human waste is discharged into rivers every year. Feargal Sharkey, former singer for The Undertones hit-making band, who went on to establish a very successful solo career and who worked as an A&R man, has retired from the music industry and become an outspoken activist doing what he can to save the British rivers and chalk-streams. Sharkey uses his twitter page to post news of sewage discharges in the rivers, as well as commenting on the extraction of water, leaving many rivers severely lacking in the amount they used to have.

The U.K. has more chalk-streams than anywhere else in the world, and they form unique wildlife habitats, suited to a wide variety of flora and fauna. Chalk-streams used to be known for the purity of their sparkling water, where aquatic plants like Water Crowfoot streamed in the current, and fish like Minnows, Bullheads and Trout were common. Today, many of these streams are filthy dirty with polluted clouded water, or even worse they have dried up completely and the stream-beds have become overgrown with weeds. Sadly, many of these rivers and streams no longer make it very far towards the sea, so at least they cannot carry any more plastic there, but it is disgusting to know that these once beautiful waterways and wildlife habitats are threatened or even no longer exist.

In rivers, some British freshwater fish, such as the Common or European Sturgeon (*Acipenser sturio*), are now in danger of extinction too, and their conservation status is Critically Endangered. Once found in large rivers in the UK, it was declared a Protected Species in 1982. Today it is only known to breed for sure in France, in the Garonne River basin. In Britain it may well be a species the country has lost by now. Sturgeon have been hunted throughout their range in Europe, because they are the source of caviar, and caviar is a very expensive food that wealthy people and gourmets want. This pattern of fish that are prized as food delicacies being sought after and caught to supply a demand is being repeated worldwide where freshwater fish and marine fish are declining fast. At the same time the rivers are being very badly polluted with chemicals, farming and agricultural waste, as well as untreated sewage.

But returning to the plastic problem, there are so many sources of plastic, in the form of microplastic, entering the rivers and streams. So many items of clothing and bedding are made from artificial fibres today, in other words plastic. Every time we wash our clothes in a washing machine vast amounts of microplastic end up going down the drain in the wastewater. I have heard that over 60% of our clothing is made from artificial fibres, and I can easily believe it. So much of our bedding is made using synthetic plastic fibres too.

Another surprising source of plastic that people often don't realise is glitter. I remember when there was a glam-rock era and glitter in makeup became fashionable then and has continued that way. The problem is though that the tiny particles of glitter, attractive as they may be, are particles of plastic, and are microplastic that has been deliberately made. When it became known that glitter was adding to the plastic pollution, a solution was found and marketed. "Eco-glitter" gives users the comfort of feeling they are not harming the planet by using this supposedly environmentally friendly alternative, but they would be wrong. An article by Sophie Hirsh, published online by greenmatters. com and entitled, "Biodegradable Glitter May Not Be as Safe as You Thought…" explains why. The article makes reference to a study in the *Journal of Hazardous Materials* conducted by Dr. Dannielle Green of England's Anglia Ruskin University. The study examines two types of so-called biodegradable glitter, and the effect they have on freshwater wildlife habitats. One form of this glitter was made from vegetable- sourced cellulose, coated with aluminium and then covered in a plastic film. Yes, you read that correctly, a plastic covering to this type of glitter. So, is it any better than regular glitter? Of course, not! It is an example of "greenwashing" to give consumers the "feel good factor" by selling them an illusion. All glitter is harmful to the environment.

Balloons are yet another big problem. Many balloons are made from plastic and even those made from natural rubber cause problems for wildlife and the environment. After a balloon is released into the air it is going to come down somewhere. It could settle on the water out at sea and get eaten by a whale or turtle. Balloons that have been "popped" are harmful too. They take a very long time to biodegrade if made from natural rubber, and if they are made from plastic this doesn't happen. Broken balloons get swallowed by wildlife, and by farm animals that graze too. Birds may incorporate a broken balloon in their nest and the chicks or the adults may get their legs tangled in what is left of the balloon. Like glitter, people think of balloons as something associated with fun, but the harmful consequences that can result from a balloon release are anything but fun!

So it goes, so frequently people do not think about how items they are using may contain plastic or about where it could end up. Another example and it is a very big one: there are countless cars, vans and lorries on the roads, but did you know that besides the air pollution they contribute to, and the roadkill and accidents that can be caused, these vehicles are another source of plastic, yes, plastic! Tyres used to be made from rubber, a natural substance, but now they are made from a mixture of rubber and plastic. As much as 24% of the makeup of a tyre today is artificial rubber, in other words, plastic polymer. Of course, over time and with the constant wear and tear on the road surfaces, the tyres will wear away into tiny dust-size particles. The plastic in them cannot decompose, and when fine like dust, gets blown away in the wind, or after a storm the water on the roads goes down the drains carrying plastic particles with it.

Some scientists today believe that even more plastic enters the seas blown there by the wind than carried down rivers. There has been a lot of talk about making new roads from recycled plastic, and it sounds a great idea at first, until you realise that this will also be adding to the microplastics in the world. Just think how many cars there are today! Plastic roads would have partially plastic tyres wearing away over them and wearing the surface of the road away too. Sometimes plastic pollution is happening without our realising it and in a way that is difficult to see. The end results are the same though. When it comes to throwing something away by throwing it in a river, when it comes to plastic there is no away!

Threats to the Oceans

Plastic pollution has probably become the most widely known threat to the oceans because it is so commonly seen and beaches have been spoiled because of it to varying degrees. However, there are many more serious dangers to the health of marine life and the composition and function of the seas. Some of them have already been mentioned but in this section, we will take a closer look at them, and the other dangers the oceans face today. You will probably be surprised how many there are.

Overfishing

Overfishing is a massive problem. Like all other unsustainable resources that we are plundering, the stocks of oceanic fish have limits and these limits are being increasingly reached. Many fish need years to reach a good size and this is no longer happening. All the big ones have been caught and not enough time is allowed for new ones to grow up and replace them. Some large fish bring a very high price and this has added to their threatened demise. Money, as usual, is a main motivator for many people in the world today, and if breaking the law means a large lump sum of money, there are those people who will be prepared to ignore legal or ethical reasons why they should not do something.

Long ago fishermen caught fish in simple nets or even on fishing lines but now there are vast supertrawlers, drift nets that are exceedingly long, and maps and technology employed to tell captains where to take their ships for easy pickings. It has been said that there are nets nowadays that are so big they could swallow a cathedral. Bottom trawlers take anything that is wanted from the lower depths and destroy a lot that is not wanted in the process. These ships are destroying millions of acres of seabed every year. It is very sadly out of sight and out of mind at the bottom of the sea. At the same time, gigantic factory ships are out there on the oceans taking and sorting and processing the riches of the seas. They really do operate as factories turning out produce. Fish and seafood are not seen as living creatures, as sentient beings, but as items to be harvested, processed and sold.

Another great danger to the marine environment that is a direct result of commercial fishing is being caused by Fish Aggregating Devices (FADs). These are floating buoys and floating objects that are tethered to the bottom of the sea by a lengthy rope, usually made from polypropylene, a form of plastic. Large plastic containers are often used as objects attached to these tethers too. It has long been known that fish are attracted to floating objects, such as pieces of driftwood, under which they can gather and shelter, so this method of fishing with FADs is using this knowledge against the fish. FADs are put in the seas to attract marlin, tuna and other highly sought after species of pelagic fish. "Fish finders" are electronic gadgets that can be attached to a FAD, and which allow fishermen to monitor the numbers of fish that have been attracted and at what depth they can be found. FADs work but it nevertheless means that large amounts of fish, including endangered species are getting caught this way. FADs are also a great danger to sea turtles and marine mammals that can become entangled in netting associated with a FAD and in lines and ropes that were used in the device's construction. Turtles, whales and seals that get tangled in nets or lines around a FAD are unable to surface to get air and the ill-fated animals drown.

Overfishing was one serious problem I was aware of but there were many more dangers to life in the seas. When I began my personal quest to do what I can to help save the oceans, and to bring awareness to other people, I realised I had better do more research. There are a lot more dangers to life in the oceans besides plastic pollution, my starting point, and that was bad enough, and overfishing, which I have just written about. There were many more ways in which the oceans are endangered, of which my knowledge had been minimal. One of the books I consulted in my research was Ian Urbina's *The Outlaw Ocean*. The author fearlessly investigates and exposes modern piracy and crime on the high seas. He takes the reader behind the scenes with the crews of the ships that are out there. He writes in depth about the poor men who are held prisoner and as slave labour on many of the fishing boats. Already from deprived backgrounds in Asia, these men are often victims of human trafficking and appalling abuse. There is not only a massive environmental problem being caused by overfishing of the oceans but there are human rights issues that lie in the background and are just as serious.

None of this fishing or overfishing would be happening if, of course, there wasn't a call for the produce, which are fish and seafood. As usual it is a case of supply to meet a demand. Although all overfishing is having a devastating effect on the life of the oceans, some forms are taking their toll quicker than others. Shark-finning, the practice of catching sharks, cutting off their fins and discarding the rest of the living creature, has brought some species to being so endangered they could become extinct unless measures are taken to counter this threat. According to the sharkstewards.org website, it has been estimated that as many as 100 million sharks are killed this way every year. Hunting sharks for their fins is a most barbaric practice, as well as being insanely wasteful. The fins are wanted to make shark fin soup, a delicacy in Asian cookery, and also the fins are used in Chinese medicine. Sadly, shark fin soup has found a market in many parts of the world in addition to where it was originally made. It is tragic to think that these amazing marine animals are killed to provide a dish for gourmets, and as an ingredient in a medicine founded on superstition.

Shark cartilage is also an ingredient in many health supplements found commonly on sale at health stores and counters. Promoted as having anti-inflammatory and anticarcinogenic properties, it has found a ready market. It has even found its way into medicines for our pets, because it is sold as a remedy for arthritis in dogs. Sadly, this means that many people are contributing to the demand for the killing of sharks because they think that the cartilage from these creatures will help them with health issues and as a way of treating illness in their canine companions. If this wasn't bad enough, shark fins contain high levels of mercury so are anything but good for the humans that consume the soup made from them. Sharks are an apex predator amongst marine life and removing them from the top of a food chain can only allow other species to thrive that would normally be eaten. Any imbalance like this causes problems elsewhere.

The fishing for tuna is another example of where overfishing has caused terrible problems. Like sharks, tuna are predatory fish, and their large size makes them an easy target, but unlike sharks, where only the fins are wanted, with tuna large specimens can sell for a lot of money. Large specimens have become increasingly rare though due to the amount that have been ruthlessly hunted. The Southern Bluefin Tuna is now in danger of becoming extinct. Most species now have an endangered status. These once very commonly found fish are being hunted out of existence.

Like with sharks, tuna tend to contain accumulated mercury, and although amounts vary, a regular diet which includes these fish is definitely not recommended. World famous entrepreneur and motivational speaker Tony Robbins became seriously ill because of mercury poisoning. He had been eating tuna and swordfish on a regular basis, thinking this high protein addition to his diet would be really good for him. It was the opposite, and he is lucky to have discovered what was wrong with him in time to have reversed the damage the mercury was doing to his body. It comes as a shock to think that someone as successful as Robbins, someone who is known for his life-improvement programmes and talks, could have lost his own due to the contamination of this toxic element that he was consuming in his food.

Because of the known problems that have been created by overfishing, fish farming in the form of inshore and offshore aquaculture was put forward as a solution. As usual, the proposed solutions sounded a great idea to begin with but when put into practice were found to cause new problems. Keeping fish in pens at sea creates the easy spread of parasites and diseases. This means that the farmed fish are doused with antibiotics or fed them in their food. Inshore farming also created a problem due to the large amount of waste products from the fish that settle on the seafloor beneath the enclosures polluting the seabed. It was thought that this problem would be avoided by offshore farming in deeper waters. Wherever the farmed fish are kept there is the risk of fish escaping and mixing with wild stock, potentially spreading disease or by interbreeding. Farmed fish are a temptation for otters and seals. After all, fish are the natural prey for these animals. This causes fish farmers to see the marine mammals as pests and this has led to killings.

Salmon farming has often contributed to the deaths of seals that have been killed in an effort to protect the farmed fish. This has been a big problem off the coast of Scotland, as just one example of where this has occurred. The salmon that is marketed after being produced at these farms is sold on to consumers using several methods to tempt the potential buyer. Images of Scotland are on the packaging and the flesh of the fish is an attractive salmon-pink or dark reddish-pink, but what the buyer doesn't realise is that often this has been produced by the use of a colouring, which can be fed to the fish in their feed. The colourings used are astaxanthin and canthaxanthin, both of which are carotenoids that normally would be obtained in the diet of wild fish from the small crustaceans that they feed on. Would so many people be tempted to buy and eat this farmed fish if they saw the conditions in which it had been kept and how it had been fed colourings to make it look attractive to the buyer?

Another big problem is that these farmed fish need to be fed on something and that something often contains a large proportion of fishmeal and fish oil that has come from the overfishing of the oceans. The fish that are mainly used to make fishmeal are herring, menhaden, capelin, anchovy, pilchards, sardines, and mackerel. These fish end up as a source of feed for farmed fish that are sold to us.

Of course, vegans and vegetarians would say that the answer to overfishing is simple: people should stop eating fish and seafood, and then there would be no problem. Getting the populations of the world to change their diets, though, is not easy. In many countries, a diet of fish has been a traditional way of life for countless generations too.

At the time of writing this book, a new film has just been released for showing on Netflix. *Seaspiracy* looks in graphic detail at some of the problems also highlighted in Urbina's book that I have mentioned above. It delves deep into the world of piracy, crime and abuse that lies behind much of the overfishing and destruction of marine life in the interests of making money and supplying the needs of consumers worldwide. This hard-hitting and controversial film is already causing some viewers to feel so upset that they are deciding to become vegan, or at least to eliminate fish and seafood from their diets. Personally, I think this documentary should be essential viewing for everybody.

If I had the ability to make a film about threats to the oceans, this would have been the kind of film I would have wanted to produce. *Seaspiracy* also reveals how much of the plastic pollution in the seas is actually from the plastic netting used by the fishing industry. Journalist George Monbiot, a speaker in the film, explains that as much as 46% of the plastic pollution is made up of netting. So why are leading campaigns against plastic pollution and environmental organisations not pointing this alarming fact out? It's all about money and business as usual. *Seaspiracy* also exposes the lies we are told about "Dolphin Safe

Tuna". Dolphins and many other marine creatures do lose their lives as bycatch in the hunt for this fish. There is no guarantee that no dolphins lost their lives in bringing a tin of tuna to you. We are being asked to take someone's word for it, some captain of a fishing boat, whose livelihood depends on selling his catch.

So, the overfishing continues as business as usual, and so does the use of vast amounts of netting and so does the plastic pollution and the destruction of marine life.

Cruise Ships and the "Magic Pipe"

Many people enjoy taking holidays and breaks on cruise ships, and going on a cruise can be a wonderful way of seeing the world. However, it is not only the ships used for trawling and fishing that are causing great problems in the oceans, because cruise liners, in addition to sometimes dumping plastic and other trash into the water, can be seriously polluting the seas with oily and contaminated bilge water. A system known as the "magic pipe" conveys the untreated wastewater directly into the oceans where it disappears, as if by magic, and the pipe can be dismantled and hidden away too. This contravenes maritime protection laws.

According to Wikipedia, on 26 August, 2013, the crew of the *Caribbean Princess* knowingly discharged 4,227 gallons of oily wastewater off the south coast of England. This was reported by an engineer who resigned his position, to the UK Maritime and Coastguard Agency. An investigation was launched into Princess Cruises and it was discovered that as many as five Princess ships had been illegally disposing of waste this way since 2005. In 2016, Princess Cruises pleaded guilty to seven charges and were given a record penalty of $40 million for their crime. This was for illegally discharging contaminated waste water off the coast of several states of North America, as well as off the U.S. Virgin Islands and Puerto Rico.

Fellow Moon Books author, Luke Eastwood in his Electric Publications book *How to Save The Planet*, also points out the harm that cruise ships can do, and he also adds container ships to the polluters. Eastwood says that both forms of ships use a "particularly dirty form of diesel fuel, which is hugely polluting...." He adds that he is sorry for being a "spoil-sport" but "taking a cruise liner is one of the worst things you can do for the planet." I agree with him and am also saying that cruise ships are bad news!

Nuclear waste dumping

Besides plastic pollution, another form of serious contamination of the seas is being caused by nuclear waste dumping. Many countries have dumped radioactive waste at sea. From 1936 through up until 1993, as many as 13 countries were using ocean dumping for radioactive waste. These waste products included both liquid and solids in various types of container. The countries involved in this nuclear waste dumping were the Soviet Union, the United Kingdom, Switzerland, the United States, Belgium, France, the Netherlands, Japan, Sweden, Russia, New Zealand, Germany, Italy and South Korea. However, and fortunately for the world, since 1993 ocean disposal of radioactive waste has been banned by international treaties. But over the years there have been many discharges from nuclear power stations. The tsunami and earthquake disaster at Fukushima in Japan has led to vast amounts of water contaminated with radiation being pumped into the Pacific Ocean. This has been going on now since 2011. Japan has just announced in 2021 that they intend to dump another 1 million tonnes of contaminated water into the sea in two years. Many conservation groups and several countries, including China, have expressed their disgust, and rightly so.

Meanwhile, for the past few years, radioactive mud, potentially contaminated with particles of plutonium, have been dredged up from near the Hinkley Power station in Somerset and taken to be dumped in the sea just a mile away from Cardiff. Campaigners, led by Welsh politician and Assembly Member

Neil McEvoy and Super Furry Animals rock musician Cian Ciaran, have been doing all they can to stop the dumping. They have been using the term "Geiger Bay," to help draw attention to the serious nature of this matter, which has been ignored and brushed aside by the Welsh government and Natural Resources Wales. McEvoy enlisted the help of scientist Professor Keith Barnham to give his professional and academic views about the dangers of this mud. The professor was interviewed and demonstrated that mud from the Hinkley Station is known to have discharged Plutonium particles, and he backed up what he was saying by showing a Westminster government document. It has been pointed out that Plutonium particles can cause cancer and that not only will the radioactive mud be washed by the tides around the coasts of Wales but that dried mud particles can be picked up by the wind and carried far inland. Many tons of the mud were actually dumped at night from a dredger despite protests by campaigners.

At last, after years of campaigning, McEvoy shared on Facebook that it has been agreed that "Nuclear Mud is not in the Welsh interest," and the dumping has been halted. There is still talk of getting rid of the mud further down the coast now on the English side of the Bristol Channel. Surely though, if it potentially contains Plutonium, it should not be being dumped anywhere?

If nuclear disasters like Chernobyl have been considered so dangerous to life that humans must be evacuated and stay out of the contaminated area, aren't we asking for trouble disposing of radioactive waste into the sea? The oceans are not a garbage dump for anything and everything we want to dispose of.

Dead Zones

Plastic pollution, and overfishing, are bringing death and destruction in their wake but another threat to marine life are aptly called "Dead Zones". These are increasingly large areas of ocean, mainly off the coasts of North America, where just about everything has died, hence the name. There is nothing alive or growing on the seabed in these areas and no shoals of fish or larger predators swimming above. Not every species of life dies, however, and, in fact, there are jellyfish species that swarm in dead zones.

These dead zones could have been included in the last chapter because they are created by pollution that is coming down rivers from farmland inland. Waste water from farms contains large amounts of fertilizers and nutrients that algae can feed on. Nitrogen and phosphorus are the main nutrients. In a natural process, known as eutrophication, the microscopic plants form algal blooms and then die creating severe depletion of oxygen as they decompose. Another term for Dead Zone, and the scientific term, is hypoxia. It means a reduced level of oxygen in the water. Marine life either dies, or if it is mobile, like fish or a sea mammal, it can leave the area. The area of once-thriving sea and seabed becomes a biological desert in the ocean.

According to the National Ocean Service (NOAA), the second largest dead zone is located in the northern Gulf of Mexico. According to Wikipedia, as many as 405 dead zones around the world were counted in a study in 2008. The largest one of all is 70,000 square kilometres. An article entitled 'Number of ocean "dead zones" doubles', published by *The Portugal News*, 32 April, 2021, reveals that United Nations secretary-general Antonio Guterres has stated that the number of "Dead Zones doubled in a decade." He went on to add that this showed a "widespread failure" of protection for the oceans. Other oceanic dead zones elsewhere in the world have been found in the Baltic Sea and the Northern Adriatic.

The dead zones are not only confined to the seas but also occur in large inland waters. The Great Lakes are suffering from this very serious problem too. Lake Erie is one of the lakes very badly affected.

As I type this, the news has been breaking of a catastrophe in Florida where a State of Emergency has just been declared, and hundreds of people evacuated, because the Piney Point Reservoir, a phosphate mine pond, has just broken, releasing its toxic and radioactive waste water into the surrounding area south of Tampa. This phosphogypsum waste was formed in the production of fertiliser but now, carrying a cocktail of heavy metals, it is on its way into Tampa Bay. Is it any wonder there are dead zones?

The ocean off the coasts of America have long been used as dumping grounds. An article for Counterpunch.org, by Evaggelos Vallianatos, entitled "Out of Sight, Out of Mind: Ecocide in the Pacific", describes how the US has dumped plutonium, lead, dioxin and pesticides in the Pacific. It reports how Professor David Valentine, of the University of California, discovered that 500,000 barrels of the banned pesticide DDT, had been dumped in the ocean near Catalina Island. The dumping began in 1947, and continued until 1982. It was described as the "most infamous case of environmental destruction off the coast of Los Angeles." With all the radioactive waste and toxic chemicals that have been disposed of in the seas, it is a wonder that so many marine species have survived, though there are now serious worries about many forms of ocean life.

Coral Bleaching

Coral bleaching is a terrible danger to a specific marine habitat. It is when coral in reefs get into very real trouble often caused by warming water, and also if the colony gets stressed due to negative changes in the light and nutrient supply. The coral polyps expel the tiny algae (zooxanthellae) that live within their bodies in a symbiotic relationship, which also produces the beautiful colours we see in the corals. When the water cools again and if conditions return to a healthy level, and if the time has not been too long, it is possible for the algae to re-enter the coral and life to continue as it was. However, if the water stays too warm for too long then disaster strikes because the coral dies after "bleaching", in other words, after losing all its colour and turning white. This has been increasingly happening in the Great Barrier Reef of Australia. You may have seen this reef featured on TV programmes narrated by Sir David Attenborough. In fact, Sir David, in the *RSA Lecture*, "People and Planet", says that the coral reefs and the fate of the oceans are one of his main concerns. He emphasises what he is saying by adding that one of his most memorable experiences was the first time he swam in a coral reef.

The amazing range of colours and shapes of the fish and other creatures that live in this and other reefs is mind-blowing in its range of diversity. In 2005, half of the coral reefs in the Caribbean were lost in a massive coral bleaching that occurred in the area. But it is not always heat that causes the problem. Cold too, a drop in temperature, can have the same devastating results. In 2010, this happened in the Florida Keys, and much of the coral in reefs there actually died after a coral bleaching event.

Climate Change is increasingly causing coral bleaching due to extreme weather bringing temperature changes that are too much for species living in an area. Another threat to the coral reefs and the coral colonies of polyps living on them comes from a very commonly used product, and this will no doubt come as a surprise to many people. Chemicals in sunscreen are a very serious danger to reefs. A report by David J. Cross, M. A., for azocleantech.com/news, looks in depth at this problem. In "Sunscreen Pollution Proves Highly Toxic to Coral Reefs," Cross explains that oxybenzone is one of the dangerous constituents of sunscreen, and it increases coral bleaching. Butylparaben, octinoxate and 4-methylbenzylidene (4MBC) are also very harmful to reefs and marine life. In 2018, Hawaii banned the use of sunscreen preparations containing oxybenzone and octinoxate, so seriously damaging are these chemicals.

The dangers of sunscreen chemical ingredients were described in a 2016 study by NOAA in the *Archives of Environmental Contamination and Toxicology*. A further study in 2013 discovered that developing coral is harmed by benzophenone-2 (BP-2), a UV filter, which besides being in sunscreens, is often present in many cosmetics, make-up brands and in soaps. With coral reefs being in danger of dying there is a serious knock-on effect because countless species of fish and other marine creatures need the reefs as spawning grounds, as areas they grow up in, and as stop-off points in migrations. A coral reef under normal conditions supports an incredible range of biodiversity, so healthy reefs are vitally important in the bigger picture of the world oceans being as they should be.

Sonar and Military Testing

Yet another serious danger to oceanic life, certainly when it comes to whales, the use of sonar and military testing has a terrible effect on these mammals. As if these majestic creatures do not already have enough dangers to contend with, from whale hunters, plastic netting, plastic waste that they may swallow, and the lack of their prey for them to catch in the overfished seas, the use of sonar by the Navy adds to their difficulties. Their sensitive hearing is literally blasted with deafening sounds, and the peace of the oceans where they communicate over very long distances is ruined. For a pod of whales this can be very alarming and disorienting. In their panic they may dive very deep to avoid the noise, or leave the area completely and lose their way having been thrown off course from their usual routes. They also may stop feeding. A report by Jack O'Donovan for the Marine Conservation Society states that "sonar technology" can have a "sudden impact on beaked whales over 25 miles away from its source." Navy sonar is employed at times in underwater research for the oil and gas industry, and this testing can go on for several weeks at a time. It is thought that military sonar causes whales to become so distressed that they end up beaching themselves. Far too many whales are dying after becoming stranded this way.

Seabed Mining

Whilst many people have been rightly protesting about the drilling for oil and gas inland and about the process of fracking for natural gas, mining of the seabed is another serious danger to the healthy state of the oceans. I am sure you have seen depressing news of oil spills from tankers that have run into trouble whilst transporting oil. There has already been far too much of this, and the threat is being extended to Arctic waters now that large areas of the seas there are opening up due to the melting ice. Drilling in the seabed anywhere is simply asking for trouble. It has been well established that we should be cutting down on our use of fossil fuels, because their usage is contributing to the Climate Crisis by adding to the greenhouse gases, so why are the seabeds being mined for them? Money is the answer as always! If there's money to be made from something then there will be greedy humans somewhere who will be after it, and prepared to do whatever is necessary to earn that money, whatever it is that has to be done! Life on Earth and consideration about the future take second place, if they are thought about at all, when there's a lot of money to be made.

There are as many as 3,400 wells in the Gulf of Mexico alone, and the gas and oil market is on the increase again despite the terrible Deepwater Horizon disaster of 2010, in which there were workers who lost their lives and an oil spill that made world headlines and ruined much of the Gulf, killing vast numbers of marine creatures and seabirds. A BP rig was responsible for the drilling and the accident. However, despite the Climate Crisis and the known danger of the world continuing to use fossil fuels, the major companies Halliburton, Diamond Offshore, TransOcean, Geoservices and Schlumberger, are all continuing to invest in mining for oil. For example, there is deepwater drilling in the Mediterranean and off the coast of East Africa. Once again it is the same old story and business as usual at the expense of life on Earth, serious damage to the environment and no consideration for the future.

Another form of seabed mining doesn't involve drilling and being fairly new is still very much in the experimental stage, with the effects it may have on marine life unknown. Seabed miners are using hydraulic pumps and bucket systems to mine areas of the seafloor around hydrothermal vents, some 1,400 to 3,700 metres deep. These vents are home to some fascinating forms of marine life, including tube worms and deep sea crustaceans. Polymetallic nodule mining takes place in shallow seas or at deeper levels, and involves the removal of nodules that are clumps of mixed metals deposited on the seafloor. Manganese, cobalt, copper and nickel are some of the main metals sought after. Suction pumps bring the potato-sized nodules to the surface where they are taken aboard a dredger. Unwanted materials are dumped back into the ocean. Plumes of sediment are created that can smother marine life on the seabed, and this is what marine conservationists are concerned about. This form of seabed mining is taking place in the Clarion-Clipperton Fracture Zone in the Central Pacific Ocean. This zone is some 4,500 miles long. Meanwhile, in the coastal waters of New Zealand, Trans Tasman Resources wants to mine off the coast of Patea in the South Taranaki Bight. They want to remove millions of tonnes of iron-sand that contains magnetite, titanium oxide and vanadium oxide. Greenpeace has been very active campaigning to stop this. The environmental organization is very worried about the potential harm to marine life there, including the endangered Maui Dolphins and the Pygmy Blue Whales that live in the area.

Climate Change

Last, but certainly not least, on the list of threats to the oceans we have Climate Change, which is causing an incredible amount of very serious problems both on land and at sea. The balance of life and the ecosystems are being thrown out of kilter by the abrupt changes in temperature. A massive and ongoing problem is being created by the melting on the polar ice and glacial melt too.

The sea levels are rising and it is obvious that civilization, as we know it, will be under threat globally, when coastal cities are in danger of flooding from the oceans. In some parts of the world this has already begun. There are Senegalese coastal villages that are now endangered by the sea, and in Wales a village on the coast has been told that the inhabitants are going to have to move at some point in the near future. Fairbourne is on the coast of Barmouth Bay and there are around 850 people living in the seaside hamlet of 400 houses. Estimates have suggested that the point of no return for the village will have been reached as soon as 2042, and Gwynedd Council, who are in charge of land in the area, have said they will not be able to continue to spend money on flooding defence and protection for Fairbourne. Yes, it is true that no one knows for sure when the sea will claim this village or if it will happen for sure but more than enough alarm bells have rung signalling its demise.

Land on the coast, including villages, towns and cities, being ruined by rising seawater is a new problem that wouldn't have been thought about until fairly recently. In addition to this, the water that has been stored on land, frozen as ice, becomes freshwater when it melts and this is causing terrible dilution of the salinity of the seas. The increase in severe storms is causing flooding on land, much of the water of which, eventually reaches the sea after being brought down the rivers. In addition to bringing vast amounts of plastic and other litter, as well as mud and silt, the rivers in storm-fueled conditions are now carrying a lot more freshwater to the seas than would normally be expected. Many marine creatures and fish are unable to live or do well in water with decreased salinity.

In some cases, the freshwater mixing in the ocean waters to decrease the amount of salt present is having a new and terrible effect on marine life. It has recently been discovered that large numbers of dolphins have become seriously ill and dying after their bodies have become covered in painful lesions. Scientists discovered that this new threat to these animals has been caused by the large amounts of freshwater entering the coastal waters, and to which they are not adapted. *The Guardian* reported on this in an article by Elle Hunt, which states that dolphins have been found off the coasts of the US, South America and Australia, suffering from a "freshwater skin disease," a form of dermatitis that has come about because of reduced salinity in the water the animals have been living in. If this is what is happening to dolphins, what other marine life are suffering because of the large amounts of freshwater entering the seas? Too much freshwater entering the seas is one of the dangers resulting from Climate Change.

There are many more problems. We have already discussed coral bleaching happening in the reefs but I am mentioning it again here because this too is a result of Climate Change causing the water of the oceans to become too warm, and it is a point worth emphasising. Global Warming means the warming of seas as well as the land, and marine life is often left struggling to survive under the new conditions it had not evolved and adapted to live in. *TheConversation.com* has reported how "Marine life is fleeing the Equator to cooler waters." The website's article explains how many species are quitting the tropical seas and moving into subtropical waters. This is causing a problem for the species already there because they may now be attacked as prey of the invaders from warmer waters or rivals for food and space. Worryingly the report also points out that history tells us that this happened before when there was a major extinction event. Could this be about to happen again? Apparently 252 million years ago at the end of the Permian period, 90% of all marine species died when the tropical seas became too warm and the creatures living in them either moved or died out.

Ocean Meadows and Forests in the Sea

There is a very real problem that has been created by modern farming with its monoculture cropping that creates "green deserts," and in many countries, including the UK, the amount of wildflower meadows has very seriously declined. This has had a knock-on effect on all the insect life that was supported by a profusion of wild species of plants. The insects have declined too, and, of course, where there are no insects there is no food for birds that normally feed on them.

So many conservationists and naturalists have been doing what they can to get wildflower meadows restored, however, there are underwater meadows that need to be thought about and protected too. Because they are under the waves, you have possibly never seen a meadow on the seabed but they do exist, and there used to be a lot more of them. There are green, grass like plants that grow on seabeds and these underwater fields provide homes and nurseries for countless species of fish and other forms of marine life. Fortunately, efforts are being made to look after some of these meadows and to plant new ones. Also known as "Prairies of the Sea," the underwater meadows are made up of large numbers of types of seagrass. There are as many as 60 different types but in the Northern Atlantic area, a species known as Eelgrass (*Zostera marina*) is the dominant type found. In tropical seas there can be many more species growing in a seagrass meadow. Up to 13 different types of these marine plants have been discovered in meadows on the seafloor. These grasses, like plants that grow on land, produce chlorophyll in their leaves, and like terrestrial plants, they have flowers and seeds. They anchor themselves to the seabed with rhizomes that spread through the substrate at the bottom of the sea, while the thin grassy leaves grow upward towards the sunlight.

These seagrass meadows are vitally important to the health

of the oceans, and by extension to the rest of the world. They are nurseries for an incredible number of fish species, as well as being home to all sorts of marine life. The biodiversity that depends on underwater meadows includes sea turtles, dugongs, seahorses, pipefish, crabs, shrimps, sea urchins and scallops. These underwater expanses of seagrass are some of the most productive marine ecosystems of the planet, and rival coral reefs for their importance as homes to the incredible range of lifeforms they support. These meadows also have so many benefits to the world at large. They are said to hold twice as much carbon dioxide per hectare as rainforests, and are therefore examples of major carbon sinks. They help remove the acidity of the seawater, as well as stabilising heavy metals polluting that water. The growth of the seagrass plants also helps prevent coastal erosion of the seabed, as well as slowing wave action and tidal currents. But it is not just at sea that these marine flowering plants have their benefits. The seagrasses have even been harvested for use as fertilizer for sandy soils. Known as "molico," they were used like this after being collected from the Aveiro Lagoon on the northern coast of Portugal.

Sadly, the underwater meadows of the oceans, like so much marine life, are in danger. They are badly damaged by pollution and by bottom trawling that rips up the seabed. It has been estimated that as much as two football fields are being lost every hour.

Realising that action needs to be taken to save and restore the underwater meadows, there are marine conservation projects underway to protect the seagrasses and get them growing well again. In America, restoration efforts have taken place in the seas of Virginia, Florida and Hawaii, and the UK is a country that has taken steps to make sure these vitally important meadows are not lost too.

Kelp Forests

As well as underwater meadows there are forests under the waves. Kelp forests are made up of very large numbers of these very large seaweeds or algae growing on the seabeds. Just like the seagrass meadows they support a large number of marine species, and have an extremely important role to play in the health of the oceans and in the lives of the many animals they support. Covering the world's underwater coastlines in many parts of the world, kelp forests form marine habitats for countless species. Shrimps, marine snails, crabs, brittle stars, and many types of fish can be found in these beds, as well as herbivorous creatures that feed on these gigantic seaweeds.

Other forms of marine wildlife that hunt in the kelp forests for their prey include whales, sea otters, sea lions, seals, and a variety of seabirds, such as gulls, terns, egrets and cormorants. The Sea Otters have often been featured in television nature documentaries because they are so cute to look at, and they have very interesting behaviour. These marine mammals demonstrate the knowledge and use of rudimentary tools.

But getting back to the kelp, the main genera are Ecklonia, Laminaria, Lessonia, Alaria and Eisenia. Laminaria is found growing on both sides of the Atlantic, as well as off the coasts of China and Japan. The Ecklonia species favour Australian waters, and also offshore in New Zealand and South Africa. Macrocystis is a main genus of kelp that grows along the northeastern and southeastern coasts of the Pacific. The greatest variety of marine biodiversity in the kelp forests is found in the northeastern Pacific from the north of San Francisco right up to the Aleutian Islands in Alaska. Most kelp forests are found in the cooler temperate and polar waters, although some of this type of marine forest was found to exist too in the tropical seas off the coast of Ecuador. And off the coast of Cape Town in South Africa is a kelp forest known as the "Great African Sea Forest." It has recently come to the world's attention because it is the setting for the Netflix film

"My Octopus Teacher," which has become a great success.

One of the main threats to the kelp forests worldwide is overfishing. You are probably wondering how this can be, so let me explain. The process of overfishing can drastically remove species of fish that are the usual predators of herbivorous marine creatures. By causing a great reduction in numbers of the predatory species an imbalance is created in which herbivores, such as sea urchin species thrive to such an extent, they can graze away so much kelp that an area becomes barren. When thinking about saving the seas, we need to think about saving the underwater forests too.

Mangrove Forests

Mangrove forests are a type of forest that covers the area between the land and water. The mangrove trees and shrubs are around 110 different species that are adapted to growing along coasts where the seawater hits and partially covers the land. The main genus is Rhizophora. Unlike most flowering trees and plants, they have evolved to tolerate high levels of salinity in the water. They are, technically speaking, halophytes, meaning salt-tolerant plants.

Mangroves grow in salt water and/or brackish water and are found in 118 countries around the world, but always in subtropical or tropical locations. The mangrove biome is known as "mangal," and consists of woodland and shrubland growing right at the edge of the sea. The mangrove trees are not only adapted to survive growing in and exposed to salt concentrations in the water but can also withstand temperature changes, as well as the low oxygen-availability of the mud they grow in.

The species known as red mangroves have stilt-like roots that hold the trees above the water, while the root part grows down into the mud and seabed. Black mangroves grow further up on higher levels of the coastal ground. They create weird root-like projections that grow upward instead of pointing down. They help the trees breathe and are known to science as pneumatophores. Many species have buoyant seeds that float in the seawater and are carried far and wide by the tides. This allows them to colonise new suitable parts of a coastline. The red mangroves are viviparous, meaning that their seeds germinate while still on the parent trees. They begin growing while still inside the fruit of the mangrove or grow out of it. They form what are known as propagules. These are seedlings that are ready to go. They drop off into the water and are carried away.

Some types of mangrove seed can remain dormant for as much as a year, and only begin to take root and grow when they are brought by chance to the right conditions. Mangroves form a really specialised marine wildlife habitat, and there are creatures that live amongst the roots and others that live in the upper parts of the trees where the branches are in the air and sunlight. You may well have seen nature documentaries that feature mud-skippers, the weird little fish that live in the muddy regions in mangrove forests, and that spend a lot of their time out of water. They live in burrows in the mud and males display by signalling with their dorsal fins. There are also many species of crab that live in mangrove forests. Barnacles, sponges, oysters, shrimps and mud lobsters are some other forms of marine life found in these weird forests. Many fish species forage around the roots when the tides bring the water in. Birds and mammals and reptiles, such as snakes and lizards, may well find homes in the upper parts of a mangrove forest.

Mangroves have an important role to play because they help prevent coastal erosion, they anchor mud and silt among the roots and they also are a barrier to storm surge and tsunamis. Sadly, though, many mangrove forests are in danger. Coastal developments destroy them. Shrimp farming is another very serious threat. It has been estimated that as many as a quarter of the world's mangroves have been lost because of these farms, with as much as 70% loss in Java, Indonesia.

The good news is that there are efforts being made to restore and regenerate mangrove forests, though we need a lot more of this type of conservation effort, just like we need more of all the other ways people are doing what they can to save the seas.

Ghost Forests

There is another type of forest that has a lot to do with the sea, although it is not one that grows in it. At least it was not meant to, but is being forced to do so by the flooding of coasts due to Climate Change and rising sea levels. There are coastal woodlands that are dying because the land they grow on is becoming increasingly flooded by the sea. The salt water kills the trees and other plants in these forests, because unlike the mangroves we have already looked at, these tree species are not adapted to withstand high levels of salt. Because the trees are actually dying, these forests are being called "ghost forests." A lot of this forest die-off is happening along the Atlantic coast of North America, with North Carolina being really badly affected. This new problem is occurring from Maine to Florida, and in some regions permanently flooded coastal ground is another "new normal". The area covered by the ghost forests is so great that they can even be seen from space. The wetlands along the coasts, too, are becoming increasingly saltier due to the seawater that is flooding them. Terrestrial plants cannot tolerate this and die, and in the woodlands, there are no new saplings growing to replace the dead and dying parent trees. Salt-tolerant shrubs, wildflowers and grasses are starting to colonise these coastal regions, as Climate Change is causing serious change to the environment and wildlife habitats.

Action We Can Take

We have taken a look at all the problems the oceans and marine life face, and it is easy to feel powerless when confronted with the scale of it all but we need to think positively despite all this. We need to think about what we can do as individuals and collectively. This part of the book is going to examine the kind of actions we can take in an effort to save the seas. Let's take a look at what we can do to help save Mother Ocean.

The consumer society is what needs to change, and change a lot. We need a paradigm shift. Right now, and as it has been, we have had global corporations, and all manner of manufacturing businesses big and small, supplying what their customers will buy. But consumers are told what to buy! Consumers are targeted by the advertisers, and the media is used by the advertisers, to convince as many of us as possible that we need to buy some new product, replace an old one or pay for some service.

Every day we are all subjected to a stream of adverts, we see them on social media, we see them in magazines and newspapers, we hear and see them on TV and radio, the streets of cities have advertising, perhaps on billboards, or perhaps handed to you as a flyer by someone paid to give out advertising materials. We may get even more through the letterbox.

If we go out to buy something we really do need, like food, for example, we are going to see countless products and items attractively and eye-catchingly displayed. If a slogan was printed on all this stuff, it would say YOU NEED TO BUY THIS! It is a form of brainwashing we are all exposed to. But it doesn't take long though, to see that a fantastic amount of the produce we are being sold is from unsustainable resources. Even worse, many gadgets, electrical devices and machinery are not made to last. They have been designed to break after a while so you will buy a new one. Even clothing is not made to last. The fashion industry is telling consumers they need to stay in fashion so they must buy new clothes to follow the current trend.

The world at large, not just the oceans, have been plundered and continue being plundered, to supply the consumer society. One thing we can all do is reduce our consumption, not only of plastic items, which are a very obvious part of the problem, but of many other products and services we think we need but don't really. It is not only the fact that so much of what we are buying is from unsustainable sources but a very great deal of it gets thrown away at some stage. Waste products and garbage are a worldwide problem on a mind-boggling scale, and as we have already seen, a lot of our rubbish, in fact anything we don't want, has a good chance of ending up in the seas. We must remember that the ocean is not a garbage dump!

Thinking about what we are buying is very important, and sometimes it is obvious that items on sale are being harvested from the oceans. For example, tourist shops often sell shells, such as conchs and whelks, and a range of jewellery made from shells and coral. Starfish and the bodies of sea urchins also get sold. Shark's teeth on necklaces and mother-of-pearl ornaments made from the shells of abalones are two more obvious ones to avoid. Species of abalone are threatened with extinction due to overfishing and the acidification of the parts of the oceans they are found.

Some products from the sea are so easy to spot. Often though, the actual sources of an ingredient in a product or its source may be concealed unless you know what to look for. Tortoiseshell hair accessories used to be made from the carapaces of Hawksbill Sea Turtles (*Eretmochelys imbricata*), and these days, all turtles are in danger and need our help. The Hawksbill's Conservation Status is Critically Endangered and the capture and trade of products derived from them is now against the law. This means that tortoiseshell combs and other tortoiseshell items should be made from artificial tortoiseshell. Sadly, this synthetic product is a form of plastic. Sometimes it seems you just can't win. Maybe we would be better off going without tortoiseshell products all together?

As mentioned earlier, sharks are in serious trouble too, but you may not realise that squalene, an ingredient for many cosmetics in the form known as squalane, can come from sharks. There is a shark genus known as *Squalus*, and squalene was originally extracted from shark liver oil. Fortunately, due to campaigns by marine conservationists, squalene is mainly extracted from vegetable sources or synthesised. Although this is good news for the sharks, it is still likely that some of this substance used by unscrupulous cosmetic firms is coming from sharks. Cod liver oil is yet another commonly sold product that has come from the seas. It is sold in all health stores and by health supplement suppliers. There is a very large demand for it, just like the very large demand for the cod it is taken from but the stocks of these fish are seriously threatened by overfishing. In conclusion, I would say that what was once alive and lived in the sea should have been left in the sea. The less consumer demand for any forms of marine life the better.

One more action many of us can take is to be a part of local beach cleanups, if, of course, there are beaches near where we live. There are countless charity and environmental conservation groups around the world organising and taking part in these efforts to clean the shorelines. See what organisations are in your area that you can find and then support their efforts. There are also individuals who do cleanups on a regular basis, and of course, collecting litter doesn't have to be only on beaches. It can be just as easily done inland, in the countryside, along roads and on riverbanks. Gathering rubbish from the environment is a valuable service to the planet wherever it is done, because not only do a lot of the plastic items, in particular, end up swept down rivers to the seas, but very many animals and birds are killed by trash they run into when foraging.

Some people and groups like to take photos and make videos of their efforts, which they can share on social media, in the hope of inspiring other people to do their bit in clearing up litter, and maybe, just maybe, to get some of the individuals who leave litter to think about their actions and stop. Of course, you need to be careful when cleaning up a beach or gathering litter inland. Gloves should be worn and litter-picking tools employed to help ensure safety.

Artists can use the trash they have collected to make sculptures and collages for display. Art classes from schools and colleges

can do likewise, and as already mentioned, I was involved with a school that did this when we went collecting plastic at a beach in Tenerife. Taking action locally is always a good idea and it can be rewarded with really great results. Jack Ellis, who founded the Wildlife and Environmental Awareness Worldwide (WEAW) organisation, took action to help the seals on beaches in the Great Yarmouth area. He designed a poster telling readers to leave seals on beaches alone, and this poster has been approved by Great Yarmouth Borough Council for distribution around the town and at the beach areas. Ellis also succeeded in getting the story of how seals were being abused on beaches published in the local press.

Now let's take a look at another way we can take action to help save the seas. Earlier in this book I mentioned how many people have been inspired to become vegans and vegetarians after watching the new film *Seaspiracy*. Adopting a plant based diet is an excellent way of taking action, not only to save the seas but to help life on this planet in general. It wouldn't be much good if I was writing a book recommending vegetarianism and veganism if I was a meat-eating, fish-eating and dairy consumer myself, but I am able to walk my talk having become vegan 15 months ago. Many other activists have made this change in their lives. Two celebrity environmentalists that I have already mentioned in this book are Captain Watson of Sea Shepherd, and Greta Thunberg, and both of them are vegan. Sea Shepherd crews are served vegan meals and the lives these activists on the high seas lead is proof that following this lifestyle is healthy.

Animal farming is one of the main causes of environmental degradation and the creation of more greenhouse gases that are driving the Climate Change. Vast amounts of rainforest are destroyed for cattle farming or to grow soya to feed farmed animals. Pollution in the form of slurry leaves factory farms and enters rivers, as mentioned earlier. The lives of billions of animals in these farms are horrific. They are not treated as sentient beings but as items of produce that are grown to meet a demand for meat. If you can't make it all the way to being vegan, it is still a great help to be reducing the amount of meat, fish and dairy in your diet. Reduction is very important. Just as we need to reduce the demand for plastic and the use of plastic, we need to reduce the demand for animal products, and when it comes to saving the oceans this, of course, means reducing the demand for fish and seafood.

Not all marine life are caught for food or for products that can be made from them and sold, some fish and marine creatures are caught for sale to the pet shops and the aquarium trade. Marine aquariums have understandably become very popular because of the astonishing colours many species of fish that live in tropical seas display. Some of them, like the gaudy clownfish, have fascinating lifestyles too because they depend on sea anemones to guard them. They have evolved so they are not harmed by the stinging cells in the tentacles of an anemone.

Many larger pet stores and all good aquarium shops have a marine section. If the sea creatures and marine tropical fish have been captive bred there isn't a problem but if they have been caught in the wild then there is. So, if we keep exotic tropical marine fish, we should find out where they have come from. While I am on the subject of aquarium fish, another point that needs making, is that unwanted fish should never be released into the sea, or freshwater habitats, if they are freshwater species. This is because doing so can introduce a species that can become invasive and can seriously unbalance the underwater ecosystem it is now a member of.

Another method of taking action is by supporting any of the many charities that are working with marine conservation issues. I will be including some of these later in this book. Speaking of charities, supporting charity shops as a customer helps the planet too. If we buy second-hand goods, we are reducing the number of items being manufactured and sold. For example, there are a large selection of second-hand clothes for sale in charity shops, and every item of clothing bought in one of these means one less bought first-hand from a clothes store, where the chances are that the item of clothing will have been made from artificial fibres or plastic that looks like wool or cotton.

Always bring your own cloth shopping bag when shopping for most items is, of course, a personal action that reduces the amount of plastic being used. Buying in bulk helps cut down on packaging as well. Taking your own food containers when eating out, containers that can be used to take home any uneaten food, is yet another way of cutting down on plastic being used. There really are lots of small actions we can take in our daily lives. Small changes in our routines that soon become habitual.

Signing petitions is one more way you can make a difference, and so can joining a protest campaign. It is true that every signature counts. Many people think that petitions are a waste of time but this is simply not true. There are petitions that get results. It is better to give it a go than do nothing. Taking part in campaigns is something you are increasingly able to take part in digitally. You can also send letters of complaint to manufacturers and other organisations, and in these letters, you can state your case and even go as far as threatening to boycott as well. People young and old are expressing their concerns, and there are an increasing number of youngsters doing so today.

Let the Children Lead Us

Greta Thunberg has become famous as an outspoken activist and environmentalist, and she first came to the world's attention when she was in her mid-teens. Ms Thunberg is now 18 but she really began inspiring youngsters worldwide when she was younger and was speaking on behalf of the children. Many others in her age group also felt a calling to take action, to attend climate strikes and protest marches and to share material on social media.

In some cases, they have become well-known for their work, and a few, like Dara McAnulty and Jamie Margolin, have even become respected authors. McAnulty has become known as a naturalist and environmental activist, and his book *Diary of a Young Naturalist* is very highly acclaimed and an award-winner. Margolin is a climate justice activist, who, aged 15, was a founder of Zero Hour climate action group. Her debut book is entitled *Youth to Power: Your Voice and How to Use It*. These young people are not only concerned about the oceans, they are worried about the threats to life on all parts of the planet. They often use the slogan: "There is No Planet B." They know if we don't look after our home world there is no future.

There has been an incredible movement on an international level of schoolchildren and teenagers doing what they can to save the planet. Often, they have spoken about how the adults have let them down by creating this nightmare, and not accepting responsibility or doing anything to help reverse matters. It is, after all, these young people's future at stake, so of course they are worried, and they are right. They are going to have to live in whatever state the world becomes in the years ahead. These young activists are an inspiration to anyone wondering what you can do.

The youngsters who have become well-known all felt an urge to get up and do something. This is also what I hope this book will do. I hope it will give you enough background information and motivation to take part in some way in saving the seas, and saving the planet. Research is important. Many of these young people have researched the issues at stake and know what they are talking about, frequently being better informed than their parents and other adults. As Ms Thunberg often has made a point of saying, what she is talking about is not her personal opinion, but is what the scientists are stating. What appear to be her words are actually the words of scientists. Following Greta Thunberg means you are following science.

At this point, I'd like to give a shoutout to my young friend Lilly Platt who has become well-known for her voluntary work cleaning up litter and speaking out about environmental issues. She shares her cleanups as photos and reports on social media, and has personally gathered over 100,000 pieces of trash. At the age of just seven she began Lilly's Plastic Pickup. Lilly has been fully supported by her Grandpa Jim, who helped inspire her efforts and has always helped with them. In 2019, she met

Greta Thunberg and both the girls were invited to a climate rally outside the European parliament in Brussels. Today, aged 13, Lilly is well-known as a British-born Dutch environmentalist, who has become the Global Ambassador for YouthMundus, Youth Ambassador for the Plastic Pollution Coalition, and Child Ambassador for World Cleanup Day. You can follow her on Facebook here: https://www.facebook.com/lillysplasticpickup/

Older people can support the younger people in their actions, and can take part in them too. For example, I attended a Global Climate Strike in Lisbon, and was wearing my This Is Zero Hour t-shirt. It really doesn't matter if you are young or old, what matters is that you do take whatever action you feel drawn to. We need to all work both as individuals and together on saving Mother Ocean and saving Planet Earth.

Organisations Helping to Save the Oceans

In this section I am including the basic details of some charitable organisations that are worth looking further into and supporting. All of them are concerned with saving the oceans. There are many more around the world, and there are often local groups you can support.

Sea Shepherd Global

Sea Shepherd is a non-profit marine conservation and anti-poaching organisation founded by Captain Paul Watson. It has many branches throughout the world and its members believe in taking direct action to save marine life and to prevent crime on the oceans. It currently operates 12 vessels, known as Neptune's Navy, which seems very apt considering my choice of Neptune/Poseidon in publicity for my Ocean Aid project. Sea Shepherd has had the support of many celebrities, including Mick Jagger, Martin Sheen, Pamela Anderson, William Shatner and Daryl Hannah.

Sea Shepherd Global
52 Alexander Boersstraat,
1071 KZ Amsterdam,
The Netherlands
Tel: +31 20 3330694
Website: http://www.seashepherd.org
Email: info@seashepherdglobal.org

Greenpeace

Greenpeace, the now internationally well-known conservation organisation, evolved out of the Don't Make a Wave Committee, which was founded in 1970. Two years later it changed its name to the Greenpeace Foundation. The original Don't Make a Wave Committee members included Dorothy and Irving Stowe, Bob Hunter, Jim Bohlen, Hamish Bruce and Captain Paul Watson. Greenpeace currently has 27 independent national or regional branches, all of which are coordinated by Greenpeace International. Greenpeace supports non-violent direct action and works with campaigns on land and sea to protect the environment and the wildlife it supports. Greenpeace had three ships called Rainbow Warrior. Greenpeace stated its goal as to "ensure the ability of the earth to nurture life in all its diversity."

Greenpeace International
Ottho Heldringstraat 5,
1066 AZ Amsterdam,
The Netherlands,
Tel: +31 20 718 2000
Fax: +31 20 718 2002
Email: info.int@greenpeace.org

Mission Blue - Sylvia Earle Alliance

"We need to respect the oceans and take care of them as if our lives depended on it.
Because they do." - Sylvia Earle

Mission Blue - Sylvia Earle Alliance, led by its founder, author, explorer, and marine biologist, Sylvia Earle, who is also President and Chairman of the organisation, is very much about exploration of the oceans, and the inspiration to protect them while we still can do so. One of its many concerns is the network of "Hope Spots," throughout the world. These are marine reservations where it is hoped that life can thrive and survive undisturbed by the dangers it faces elsewhere.

Website: http://mission-blue.org

Marine Conservation Society

Marine Conservation Society, as its name suggests, is a UK charitable organisation concerned with taking action to save and protect the seas and the marine life in them. Campaigns have included "Beachwatch," involving beach cleanups and surveys, and "Don't Let Go," to stop the release of balloons and sky lanterns. Chris Packham and Iolo Williams are celebrity ambassadors for this organisation.

Marine Conservation Society
Overross House,
Ross Park,
Ross-on-Wye,
Hereford
HR9 7US
Website: http://www.mcsuk.org/
Email: info@mcsuk.org

Ocean Cleanup

Ocean Cleanup is an organisation founded in 2013 by Boyan Slat at the age of just 18. As a very concerned teenager, Slat was determined to take action to save the seas from plastic pollution and came up with a way of doing so. Ocean Cleanup is a non-profit organisation that is developing technologies to rid the oceans of plastic pollution, and to stop much of it entering them from rivers.

Ocean Cleanup
Batavierenstraat 15,
4-7th Floor,
3014 JH Rotterdam,
The Netherlands.
Website: http://theoceancleanup.com

Surfers Against Sewage

Surfers Against Sewage, as its name suggests, is very much about stopping the pollution of the seas with sewage but also any other form of pollution. The organisation holds beach cleanups and many other campaigns to help ensure healthy seas around the UK. It has branches throughout Britain and also in Northern Island.

Surfers Against Sewage Limited
Unit 2, Whale Kitty Workshops,
St. Agnes, Cornwall,
TR5 0RD
Website: http://www.sas.org.uk
Email: info@sas.org.uk

Blue Planet Society

Blue Planet Society is a self-funded volunteer pressure group that campaigns to stop the exploitation of the oceans. This group sells a range of merchandise including t-shirts and I am the proud owner of one that says "STOP PLASTIC POLLUTION!"

They have had a lot of success in influencing celebrities to take part in campaigns and in 2020, rock star and singer Robert Plant pulled out of a festival in the Faroe Islands after listening to what the group had to say about the Grindadrap.

Website: http://blueplanetsociety.org
Email: blueplanetsociety@hotmail.com

The Marine Diaries

The Marine Diaries is an organisation dedicated to increasing ocean literacy. It run awareness campaigns highlighting the ocean's influence on people and develops educational materials.

Website: https://www.themarinediaries.com/
Email: https://www.themarinediaries.com/contact

Suggested Further Reading

De Rothschild, D., 2011, *Plastiki Across the Pacific on Plastic: An Adventure to Save Our Oceans*. Chronicle Books, San Francisco.

Earle, S., 2014, *Blue Hope: Exploring and Caring for Earth's Magnificent Ocean*. National Geographic.

Eastwood, L., 2019, *How to Save The Planet 10 Simple steps that can change the world*. Electric Publications, Kerry, Ireland.

Lovelock, J., 2016, *Gaia: A New Look at Life on Earth (Oxford Landmark Science)*, Oxford University Press.

Margolin, J., 2020, *Youth to Power: Your Voice and How to Use It.* Hachette Go.

McAnulty, D., 2020, *Diary of a Young Naturalist*. Little Toller.

Santos, Prof., A., 2005, *Atlantis, The Lost Continent Finally Found*. Atlantis Publications.

Solibello, F., 2019, *SPAM - Stop Plastic A Mare*, Monadori Libri S.p.A. Milan, Italy.

Watson, P., 2020, *Dealing with Climate Change and Stress.* Independently published.

About the Author

Steve Andrews is a man of many talents. He is a writer, journalist, singer-songwriter, poet, naturalist and activist who has written three books on herbs and contributed to many publications. Born in Cardiff, Wales, he is also known as the Bard of Ely and Green Bard and has performed on TV and at festivals around the world including Glastonbury and Green Man. Steve now lives in Sesimbra, Portugal and devotes much of his time to ecological activism and highlighting the plight of the world's oceans.

Other books in the *Earth Spirit* series

Belonging to the Earth
Nature Spirituality in a Changing World
Julie Brett
978-1-78904-969-5 (Paperback)
978-1-78904-970-1 (e-book)

Confronting the Crisis
Essays and Meditations on Eco-Spirituality
David Sparenberg
978-1-78904-973-2 (Paperback)
978-1-78904-974-9 (e-book)

Eco-Spirituality and Human–Animal Relationships
Through an Ethical and Spiritual Lens
Mark Hawthorne
978-1-78535-248-5 (Paperback)
978-1-78535-249-2 (e-book)

Environmental Gardening
Think Global Act Local
Elen Sentier
978-1-78904-963-3 (Paperback)
978-1-78904-964-0 (e-book)

Healthy Planet
Global Meltdown or Global Healing
Fred Hageneder
978-1-78904-830-8 (Paperback)
978-1-78904-831-5 (e-book)

Honoring the Wild
Reclaiming Witchcraft and Environmental Activism
Irisanya Moon
978-1-78904-961-9 (Paperback)
978-1-78904-962-6 (e-book)

Saving Mother Ocean
We all need to help save the seas!
Steve Andrews
978-1-78904-965-7 (Paperback)
978-1-78904-966-4 (e-book)

The Circle of Life is Broken
An Eco-Spiritual Philosophy of the Climate Crisis
Brendan Myers
978-1-78904-977-0 (Paperback)
978-1-78904-978-7 (e-book)

**MOON
BOOKS**

PAGANISM & SHAMANISM

What is Paganism? A religion, a spirituality, an alternative
belief system, nature worship? You can find support for all these
definitions (and many more) in dictionaries, encyclopaedias, and
text books of religion, but subscribe to any one and the truth will
evade you. Above all Paganism is a creative pursuit, an encounter
with reality, an exploration of meaning and an expression of the
soul. Druids, Heathens, Wiccans and others, all contribute their
insights and literary riches to the Pagan tradition. Moon Books
invites you to begin or to deepen your own encounter, right here,
right now.

If you have enjoyed this book, why not tell other readers by
posting a review on your preferred book site.

Journey to the Dark Goddess
How to Return to Your Soul
Jane Meredith
Discover the powerful secrets of the Dark Goddess and transform your depression, grief and pain into healing and integration.
Paperback: 978-1-84694-677-6 ebook: 978-1-78099-223-5

Shamanic Reiki
Expanded Ways of Working with Universal Life Force Energy
Llyn Roberts, Robert Levy
Shamanism and Reiki are each powerful ways of healing; together, their power multiplies. *Shamanic Reiki* introduces techniques to help healers and Reiki practitioners tap ancient healing wisdom.
Paperback: 978-1-84694-037-8 ebook: 978-1-84694-650-9

Pagan Portals – The Awen Alone
Walking the Path of the Solitary Druid
Joanna van der Hoeven
An introductory guide for the solitary Druid, *The Awen Alone* will accompany you as you explore, and seek out your own place within the natural world.
Paperback: 978-1-78279-547-6 ebook: 978-1-78279-546-9

A Kitchen Witch's World of Magical Herbs & Plants
Rachel Patterson
A journey into the magical world of herbs and plants, filled with magical uses, folklore, history and practical magic. By popular writer, blogger and kitchen witch, Tansy Firedragon.
Paperback: 978-1-78279-621-3 ebook: 978-1-78279-620-6

Medicine for the Soul
The Complete Book of Shamanic Healing
Ross Heaven
All you will ever need to know about shamanic healing and how to
become your own shaman...
Paperback: 978-1-78099-419-2 ebook: 978-1-78099-420-8

Shaman Pathways – The Druid Shaman
Exploring the Celtic Otherworld
Danu Forest
A practical guide to Celtic shamanism with exercises and
techniques as well as traditional lore for exploring the Celtic
Otherworld.
Paperback: 978-1-78099-615-8 ebook: 978-1-78099-616-5

Traditional Witchcraft for the Woods and Forests
A Witch's Guide to the Woodland with Guided Meditations and
Pathworking
Mélusine Draco
A Witch's guide to walking alone in the woods, with guided
meditations and pathworking.
Paperback: 978-1-84694-803-9 ebook: 978-1-84694-804-6

Wild Earth, Wild Soul
A Manual for an Ecstatic Culture
Bill Pfeiffer
Imagine a nature-based culture so alive and so connected,
spreading like wildfire. This book is the first flame...
Paperback: 978-1-78099-187-0 ebook: 978-1-78099-188-7

Naming the Goddess
Trevor Greenfield

Naming the Goddess is written by over eighty adherents and scholars of Goddess and Goddess Spirituality.

Paperback: 978-1-78279-476-9 ebook: 978-1-78279-475-2

Shapeshifting into Higher Consciousness

Heal and Transform Yourself and Our World with Ancient Shamanic and Modern Methods

Llyn Roberts

Ancient and modern methods that you can use every day to transform yourself and make a positive difference in the world.

Paperback: 978-1-84694-843-5 ebook: 978-1-84694-844-2

Readers of ebooks can buy or view any of these bestsellers by clicking on the live link in the title. Most titles are published in paperback and as an ebook. Paperbacks are available in traditional bookshops. Both print and ebook formats are available online.

Find more titles and sign up to our readers' newsletter at
http://www.johnhuntpublishing.com/paganism
Follow us on Facebook at https://www.facebook.com/MoonBooks
and Twitter at https://twitter.com/MoonBooksJHP